**B♭ Trumpet**

# Easy Great Hymns

*Instrumental Solos for the Intermediate Soloist*

## Contents

**CURNOW** MUSIC

Exclusively Distributed By

**HAL•LEONARD** CORPORATION

7777 W. BLUEMOUND RD. P.O. BOX 13819 MILWAUKEE, WI 53213

Selected by James Curnow

**Easy Great Hymns**
**B♭ Trumpet**

Arranged by:
*Stephen Bulla*
*Douglas Court*
*James Curnow*
*Paul Curnow*
*Timothy Johnson*

Order number: CMP 0866-03-400
ISBN 978-90-431-1948-1
CD number: 19-043-3 CMP

# Easy Great Hymns

## INTRODUCTION

This collection of hymns includes some of the most famous hymns in the history of the church. It includes tunes that are literally from around the world. The arrangements have been created by some of the foremost writers of instrumental music, who are internationally known for their musical compositions and arrangements. The goal of these arrangements is to allow the instrumentalist the opportunity to give praise and adoration to God through their musical abilities.

There is a separate piano accompaniment book available. This accompaniment book will work with all of the soloist books. When an accompanist is not available, the accompaniment CD (included) can be used for performance. This CD will also allow the soloist to rehearse on their own when an accompanist is not available.

The accompaniment CD contains tuning notes at the beginning to allow the soloist to adjust their intonation to the intonation of the compact disc accompaniment. Each arrangement in this collection includes a sample performance with soloist as well as a track with just the accompaniment.

May you enjoy using this collection and find it useful in extending your musical ministry.

Kindest regards,

James Curnow
President
Curnow Music Press, Inc.

# 1. COME THOU ALMIGHTY KING
## Italian Hymn

**Felice de Giardini**
Arr. **James Curnow** (ASCAP)

Track: 3 13

# 2. WHEN I SURVEY THE WONDROUS CROSS
## Hamburg

**Lowell Mason**
Arr. **Timothy Johnson** (ASCAP)

# 3. FOR THE BEAUTY OF THE EARTH

Track: 5 15

Dix

**Conrad Kocher**
Arr. **Douglas Court** (ASCAP)

CMP 0866.03 B♭ Trumpet

# 4. IMMORTAL, INVISIBLE

St. Denio

Traditional Welsh Melody
Arr. **Stephen Bulla** (ASCAP)

Copyright © 2003 by **Curnow Music Press, Inc.**

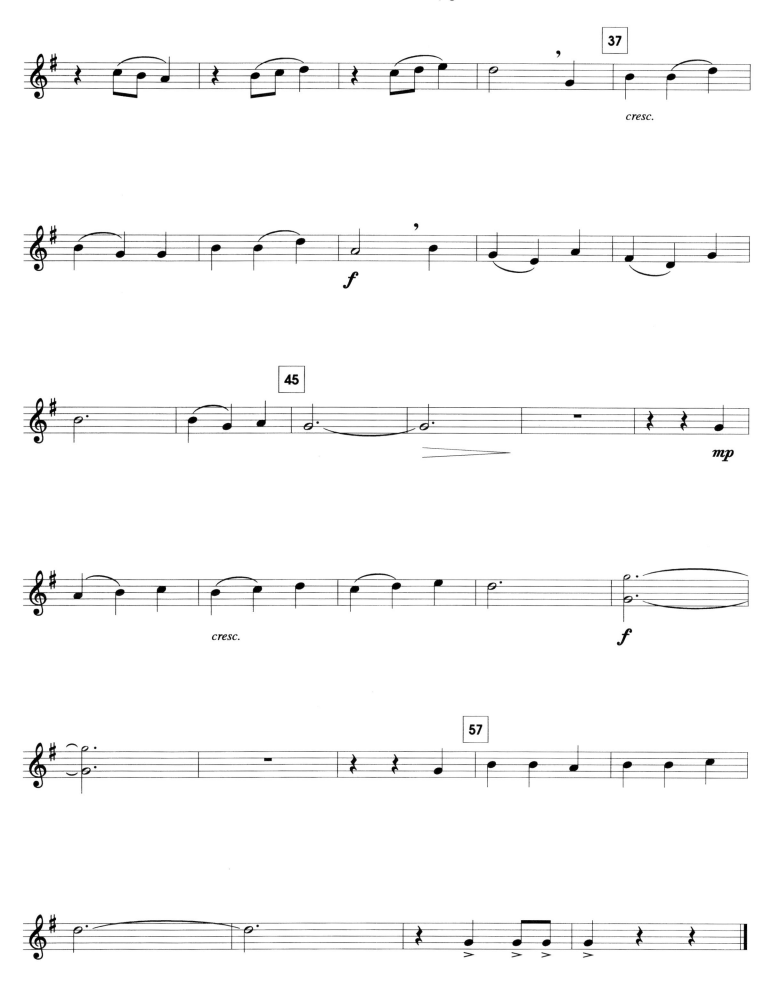

# 5. WHEN PEACE LIKE A RIVER

## It Is Well With My Soul
### Ville Du Havre

Philip P. Bliss
Arr. **James Curnow** (ASCAP)

# 6. COME, YE THANKFUL PEOPLE, COME

## St. George's, Windsor

George J. Elvey
Arr. **Paul Curnow** (ASCAP)

# 7. O WORSHIP THE KING
## Lyons

**Johann Michael Haydn**
Arr. **Timothy Johnson** (ASCAP)

# 8. TO GOD BE THE GLORY

**William H. Doane**
Arr. **Douglas Court** (ASCAP)

# 9. CROWN HIM!
## Diademata

**George J. Elvey**
Arr. **Paul Curnow** (ASCAP)

18

# 10. FAIREST LORD JESUS
## Crusader's Hymn

Traditional
Arr. **Stephen Bulla** (ASCAP)

**Tranquil and flowing** ( ♩ = 72 )